HF482029

In the beginning God created the heavens and the earth. (Gen. 1:1 KJV)

This story combines the wonder of the solar system with a biblical perspective, emphasizing the idea of a purposeful creation. It's a tale that can inspire children to look up at the night sky with awe and curiosity.

God's Great Design

Written by: Jill Craven

Once upon a time, in the vast
expanse of the universe, there
was a beautiful solar system
created by the Great Designer,
God. Each planet had its own
special role, and they all lived in
harmony, circling around the
bright and life-giving sun.

Mercury, the messenger, was the swiftest of all, zipping around the sun, delivering messages from God to the other planets.

Venus, the shining one, sparkled

with a beautiful glow, reminding

the planets of God's love.

Earth was the chosen one, filled

with life and beauty, and it was the

only planet with a blue sea and

green land. It was home to many

creatures, and God loved it dearly.

Mars, God stood watch with its

shield of red dust, always ready to

guard the solar system.

Jupiter, the giant, was the strongest of all, with its massive size and swirling storms. It was like a mighty guardian appointed by God to watch over the smaller planets.

Saturn wore a crown of dazzling

rings, a symbol of God's promise

to always be with them.

Uranus danced on its side,

spinning in a unique way, showing

that God's creations were full of

surprises.

Neptune was the dreamer, with its deep blue color, it whispered secrets of the farthest reaches of the solar system.

And then there was Pluto, the little

one, who despite being so far

away, was still an important part of

God's plan.

Together, they all formed a family,

each with their own purpose, all

part of a grand design. They were

a testament to the creativity and

majesty of God, the great

designer, who had set them all in

motion with just a word.

And every night, children on Earth would look up at the stars and be reminded of God's work, learning that they, too, were part of something much bigger and more beautiful than they could imagine.